Sugar So Sweet

Sugar So Sweet

Poems

by

Candis Yeah

Copyright © 2014 by Candis Yeah

All rights reserved.

No part of this publication may be reproduced, distributed, or transmitted in any form or by any means, including photocopying, recording, or other electronic or mechanical methods, without the prior written permission of the publisher, except in the case of brief quotations embodied in critical reviews and certain other noncommercial uses permitted by copyright law. For permission requests, write to the publisher, addressed "Attention: Permissions Coordinator," at the address below.

Published by YeahWrite Publishing
P.O. Box 1718
Stone Mountain, Georgia 30086

www.yeahwritepub.com

ISBN-10: 0615967256
ISBN-13: 978-0615967257

Printed in the United States of America

To those who know the stories behind my scars.
To those who know what Chaka Zulu meant to me.
To the one who loves me enough to allow me to exist in outer space, while keeping me tethered to Earth.
To the woman who calls me her Sweet Candy.
To the man who most understands and revels in my greatness.
To the kindred spirits that share my blood and were predestined to walk with me through this life.
For the greatest of all the gifts you all have given me is love.
And for that I am forever indebted to you.

-Yi-Yah

Granules

1	Rebuilt
2	Redwoods
6	Misgiven
8	Autumn Sprung
13	No Man Knows the Hour
14	Consumed
17	Revolution
18	God Absolute
20	The Noose Tightens
22	Letting Go of Fantasy Isle
24	Child of the Ghetto
25	Confrontation
26	I Love Me
28	Mirage
30	No One Believes
32	And in My Whirled
33	Just Beyond the Clouds
34	Free Style

35	My Piece of God on a Sunday Morning
36	Insanity Plea
39	Warring
40	Hardened
41	An Ode to My Grandma Dorothy
43	Unconcealed Cycle
45	Sunshine in the Mourning
47	Armor
49	Failure v. Success
51	DrugLord
54	Job Justified
55	Me in My Own Space
56	And for That, I Love You
58	A Birthday Poem for Snook and Outlaw
61	Venom
62	Anonymous
63	Sacrifice

Sugar So Sweet

Rebuilt

Lost…
Drifting…
In an open space

Naked…
Vulnerable…
Shamed and disgraced

Squander…
Folly…
Standing ever so still

Discovery…
Acceptance…
The cracked dam spill

Spirit…
Strength…
Self-perception unwound

Revelation…
Redemption…
New purpose found

Redwoods

The pain grows so tall.

Sequoia sempervirens,

shade your reality,
blocking the light of rationality,
providing you excuses for the drugs,
for the disregard.

Mind altering, soul numbing,
you're no longer afraid of the vipers,
or the black widow's web woven to trap you.

Tangled.

Fuck, the world,
too heavy on your shoulders,
you're just flesh,
mud from dirt, giving way.

Promised by libelous zealots that
God would not overly burden you.

Misled.

And when you stagger to truth,
you're left open and vulnerable,
scars exposed,
but your bones are breaking.

Primitive behavior,
you just have to keep living,
in survival mode.

"Iris" lyrics pour from your eyes,
in your madness,
your true colors kaleidoscopic, flashy.

Redwoods,

majestic and resilient,
an aspiration too lofty for a mortal
so fragile.

You grew from the same soil,
yet they are so much stronger than you,

withstanding storms,

heavy winds,

ominous clouds,

they will be there long after you are gone.

Those fortunate minstrels,

not burdened with feeling,

get to be free and proud,

not human,

not flawed.

Your former self,

drifting in your vast subconscious,

calls to you, pleading,

but you ignore it.

Pills swallow easier than truth,

smoke easily inhaled,

as blackened lungs pay the price

for your dark days.

Contemplating "Landslide,"

you answer no to all the questions posed,

yet the melody is so intoxicating,

you put it on repeat,

as it forces you to face your mortality.

Redwoods,

are always at the bottom of the bottle,
visible only after the last sip,
after the last hit.

When you climb to the top of them,
you are able to see the world clearly,
though abstract,
it is more real than any place you have ever known.

Misgiven

Barren.
A desolate wasteland.
Once filled with such promise,
now lies lifeless and forgotten.
I had been robbed.

I'm not sure how they slipped in undetected.
Maybe I had unknowingly let them in.
Maybe they had been there all along, hiding.
They entered through my womb and somehow
managed to leave with a piece of my heart.

They carried my gift away,
but left its wrapping
and the fabricated joy it elicited.

My dreams fell from between my legs,
mangled and unrecognizable.
Unforgiving steel that looked like
death in its tangible form,
devoured traces of my womanhood.

I'm bleeding. I'm hurt mama.

You've always protected me,
yet I stood by and did nothing
while they took my gift from me.

Weak.
Strong arms and kind words offer support,
but they cannot reach me
because I'm not here right now.

I'm out looking for the bastards that robbed me.

Autumn Sprung

I watched an old
woman, perched in her window,
hands folded in front of her,
as longsuffering tears traced
the wrinkles on her face.

She began praying for the world
that turned before her, wondering
how a creation born
with Edenistic ambitions
had come to a state of such disrepair.

War, a more worthy investment
than the decaying schools
that taught young
soldiers to die.

A world pulsating with
the intoxicating music of the
once downtrodden who have
risen to decimate others.

A black-faced minstrel show.

A world illuminated
by calculatedly vulgar
images streaming from televisions
that have morphed
into idols worshipped
by even the lowliest of beings.

Pale faces with full bellies,
scoff as babies beget babies
in forgotten slums,
and would-be grandmothers destroy
mistakenly-fertilized seeds
that would have grown
to tarnish suburban purity.

Young minds raped by
a society chasing profit,
it's prophetic
as mothers turn against daughters,
and wing-tipped vultures
behind desks become wealthier.

A world in which a rainbow
draws colorful lines that separate
one human being from another,
lines that are difficult to conceal or ignore.

Manmade religious dogmas
are daggers, sharp and thirsty
for blood as extremists
are emboldened by beliefs
that every Babylonian sinner
must be made to atone for his transgressions.

Bombs crafted in hidden lairs,
enemies burrow closer to the hell
where their souls will join Sisyphus on
his forsaken quest for eternity.

An eternity that minces
rights and wrongs into a mound
of vegetative nonsense
that, if digested, will cause
its consumer to explode
in a crowded shopping center.

I study the old woman
as she petitions her
God for redemption.

White hair caresses her shoulders,
skin weathered by many days,
hands that had touched people
she remembers now only in her dreams,
tired eyes that have borne witness
to things that the generations after her
cannot fathom as truths.

So entranced by the woman's
simple robe, I did not notice
a car park in front of her house.

By the time I'd realized it, the strangers
were walking toward her door,
bags draped uneasily over the hurried male,
while the female walked purposefully
behind him carrying a white bundle.

I was startled when the package
wrapped tightly in her arms
began to move.

A baby!

The old woman eagerly
greeted her guests,
and returned to the window smiling,
holding the baby, proudly
displaying it to the world
or maybe to the God
to whom she had been praying.

Thank God for new beginnings

No Man Knows the Hour

I got high
on the day the world
was supposed to end,
I needed to be closer to God
in case of an emergency.

My love and I
lied on the grass,
trading secrets
as we watched the sky.

It was a peculiar color
that night and we imagined
we would be sucked into a swirling
cloud that was sure to descend from it,
but the cloud never came.

Nothing exciting ever happens around here.

Accepting that our interpretation
of ancient mystics
had been wrong, we went inside
and made love as if
it would be the last time.

Consumed

I was consumed

Hot coals under my feet

Needles pricking my fingers

Tumbleweeds in my gut

I was consumed

Great risks and lives laid down, produced skyscrapers of intellect in my mind

A beautiful skyline in testament to God's divinity and mankind's capability

But when I climbed to the top of the highest point and peered out of the window

I could only see a blanket of white fog, the overcast had set in so thick

I was consumed

Spiders running through my veins

Scratches on a chalkboard

Metal against teeth

I was consumed

Sometimes the straitjacket would squeeze so tight, I could hardly breathe
The padded walls shaped an environment much different than that of my heart
A place where organized anarchy was ruler
And Godzilla wreaked havoc in a language I could only understand in my dreams

                    I was consumed
                Waves crashing to shore
                Sunrays after an eclipse
                Absolute edge of the cliff
                    I was consumed

I chose not to be strong, flesh cannot be concrete
I folded like paper, bones can always mend
A fiend addicted to the sensation flowing through me
I hid my face as my neglected spirit paced angrily within me
How naïve to trust my senses, gateways to weakness

　　　　　　　　I was consumed
By his thoughts and philosophies spoken ever so eloquently
By the love that bound him to me making it implausible to separate
By his touch that enwraps me even now at the remembrance of it
　　　　　　　　I was consumed

Revolution

Revolution is thick in the air, hot on the heels of the oppressors

Unnerving those who've created countless martyrs for generations

Blood of uprisers lies unclaimed in the streets, its striking redness fierce against the sandy backdrop

The sand is neutral, but the blood cries out in protest, unwilling to be silenced

A generation of fools, incited by the ever-shrinking world, possessed the audacity to dream of a better existence for its people

Utilizing the same technology that invites many into a cultural phenomenon of stupidity, they are changing the face of history

Dark skin can contend with devastating sunrays and has a knack for surviving the harshest of conditions

It also has a great propensity for rebelling against normalcies set up to contain the power that lies beneath its surface

The nose of the Sphinx is still absent, but the face of a land has gained a new appendage

God Absolute

I cannot trade hood tales with him,
his hands are soft from a life of privilege,
but he has suffered.

Foolishly, he tried to rationalize
the endless nature of the universe,
and the complexities of the unknown
drove him mad.

In his insanity, he found comfort
in cocaine that caused his heart
to beat in sync with the anxiety
that plagued him.

Ever shadowed by silent anticipation
as if a stranger would walk through
the door at any moment;
a door visible only to him.

Tortured by the conundrum
that he could *feel* God,
but could not *touch* God.

Something must be tangible
in order to be real, right?

He was real, as his heart
exploded inside of him,
but he did not die.

That must have been God, right?

He escaped bullets and prison,
those gross contradictions
to his exceptional intellect
and proud upbringing.

Favor preserved him
and love beckoned him
back from the brink
as he made peace with fears
that ignite war, and found solace
in unanswered questions.

God, right.

The Noose Tightens

They're no longer hangin' us from trees,
But now hangin' us from degrees,
They won't kill us 'cause they're after our seeds,
Carrying them away on a stiff breeze.

On top of the playground they build a prison,
From the cradle to the cell they send our children.

They rope the noose of capitalistic gain tight around our necks,
We're tangled in the tree of living from check to check,
Bangin' our heads against the walls of debt,
Beatin' our chests crying for respect,
We ain't in slavery, but we feelin' the effect.

Some of our babies are born craving cooked crack,
With stereotyped knives stuck in their backs,
Sacrifices lying tied to the train tracks.

Sunrays of wealth are shining, but we're shaded from it,
While their sun-screened faces soak up profit,
We've chosen not to wade in endless oceans,
instead wallow in shit,

Make-believe advancements pretend to be legit,
Some still cry out, others have quit,
Ignorant of our power, we create puns with no wit.

The noose is tightening, shortening our breath,
We must educate ourselves and resist
while there's still air left.

Letting Go of Fantasy Isle

I've had several lovers since I last had you,
A few walks on the beach, a few sunsets too.

I've been to the moon, Mars and back,
Hunted proudly with lionesses, ran with a wolf pack.

I've kissed the top of Mount Kilimanjaro,
Put off what I could do today for tomorrow.

I've sauntered through a field of lilies, then stopped to smell the roses,
Traversed a savannah and saw animals striking curious poses.

I've fought in battles with the most fearless knights,
Marched united on segregated streets with blacks and whites.

I've been to heaven and danced on pavement of gold,
Acquired calculated wisdom from those who've grown old.

I've created fire without the aid of a spark,
Burned quietly at the stake with Joan of Arc.

I've learned all of the languages spoken worldwide,
Stood in front of a mirror and beamed with pride.

I've conquered my worries, set aside my fears,
Grew a garden more impressive than the Queen's with my tears.

I've gone back into the womb and been birthed again,
Washed myself guiltless and free of sin.

I've joked with Pryor and laughed amongst kings,
Stroked the Sphinx and decoded ancient writings.

I've done all the things my mind has dared to do,
Let go of memories, let go of you.

Child of the Ghetto

I'm a child of the ghetto,
A seed of the struggle,
Wondering what woes await me tomorrow.
Wondering how I will overcome,
Wondering how I can be like the one…who made me.
This perfect being,
Bred into an imperfect society.
I will be that optimistic leaf that says yes!
And change a forest full of no,
Yes, me, this simple child of the ghetto.

Confrontation

The more your heart breaks
the less afraid
of the dark you become

Nightlight turned off
and the voices from the
television no longer offer comfort

Just blackness
with traces of the moon
slipping in

Submitting to various primal
needs requires lying down
but you're tired of being on your back

So you have no use for sleep
as you battle your demons
and confront your heartbreak
standing up

I Love Me

I love me 'cause me loves I,

I'm the writer and singer of my own lullaby,
which soothes my soul when life's awry,
sending my spirit soaring high,

I'm in control of my own life.

My destiny is steered by me,
fate can't even deter she,
she is I and I is me,

I dance in the eye of the storm.

I taunt misfortune, daring it to rear in my direction,
nay, I say unto you misfortune,
for you do not exist in my reflection.

I love me 'cause me loves I,
I wipe my own tears when I cry.
Tears do not flow uncontrollably,
I use them to flush weakness from my body.

My body is mine, owned by me,
which is ruled by we,
my soul and I that is,
we are one,
my soul and I that is.

So, since she is I and I is me ruled by we,
my soul controls everything,
therefore, I must keep it pure, honest and clean.

My soul is governed by my conscience,
which I'm guilty of sometimes ignoring,
yet with help from God, I'll continue to write my own story.

I love me 'cause me loves I.

Mirage

All this time I'd been walking around
like I'm special,
floating above the Earth,
denying all of her wares,
mirages she tried to sell me.

I'm too smart for that,
too enlightened,
too prized by God.

But now that the pain
has grown so tall,
mountainous before me,
I realize I am weak.

It wasn't until, embarrassed,
my blood ran from me onto the floor,
that I discovered I bleed
red like everyone else.

I've been deserted,
I can't feel you right now
and that unsettles me.

You were in the womb with me,
now I've chased you off.

Disgraced, I'll never get my wings back,
you'll never reclaim me. Useless.

Guess you wanted to drive
home your point, but
why not take the house,
the clothes, the car?
Why take my inspiration?

I already know you're
bigger than me,
amongst the few who understand
I am a mere speck of dust
to be blown away in time.

All I've thought myself to be
has been wrong, and I'm crumbling
so easy between your finger and your thumb.

Even still, please don't take your hand from me.

No One Believes

Morning is dawning in a routine of bittersweet irony,

The sun is shining, yet the world is dark,
Ignored, mighty Gabrielle demands, "Hark!"
But no one believes in angels anymore.

The voyage of a dove interrupted by a bullet,
Shot down because
No one believes in peace anymore.

A forgotten child dies in a gutter,
No one mourns because
No one believes in the future anymore.

Wars waged based on false prophesies,
No smoke billows in protest because
No one believes in justice anymore.

Politicians peddle fantasy,
No one votes because
No one believes in the government anymore.

People tread on their brethren,
Sinful, unrepentant hearts because
No one believes in humanity anymore.

Stock no longer invested in hope or faith,
We find it hard to believe in anything because
We no longer believe in ourselves.

And in My Whirled

My fictional world has consumed my reality,
    and I'm having trouble separating truths

Make-believe lovers smile at me,
    and I'm swimming through abstract views

Can't figure which way is up nor which is down,
    ever mocked by strategic blockades

Led into the parted Red Sea to drown,
    invisible wounds, transparent Band-Aids

My imaginary world is safer to dwell in,
    no bullets, wars, or magical beans

There's honor, valor, and righteous doctrine,
    justice for all by any means

I surrender to the serenity of this world in stride,
    swaying with its winds, for they are my guide

Just Beyond the Clouds

Joy will come, just wait
You can always find happiness, it's never too late

Cling to faith and never let go
God is your life raft and will keep you afloat

He knows your needs and has not forgotten you
Just beyond the clouds the sun is shining through

Free Style

We allergic to jobs
Yo, that would be the death of us

9-to-5 cubicle pods
Just like the rest of us

They know we are hard
But they stay testing us

They see we are stars
But they keep oppressing us

We give it to God
Because He be protecting us

My Piece of God on a Sunday Morning

I loved you from the first moment my eyes met yours
Silly of me to believe in love at first sight
But I was just a girl then
And girls dream in fairytale
No prince charming for me
Just you
Flawed and beautiful
You had sojourned through Hundred Schools of Thought
And that impressed me
You painted colorful images in my mind with words
And that pleased me
Our love, a plum blossom, bloomed in a Warring State
Vibrant against the snow
A harbinger of the impending spring

Insanity Plea

This shit comes so easy to me,
it oozes from my veins,
flows like the blood from the
      self-induced slits
        in my mental wrists.

I'm going insane,

I'm like the red tip
of a blind man's cane.

All recognize my search
as I taste the concrete,
      led by heightened senses
        and entities so discrete.

My ocean is a bottomless pit
where at any depth light manages to seep,
      or is it simply my flooded imagination
        telling me I'm that deep.

I'm open, you don't have to dig
to find my person,
>   for all of my buried treasures
>   lie vulnerable on the surface.

I run swiftly, but I often
stumble and fall,
>   because I never bothered
>   to first learn to crawl.

Sometimes the darkness screams
as loud as the light,
>   sometimes the sun
>   must tuck me in at night.

I offer my peace pipe,
but its recipients only choke,
>   their lungs can't be fooled
>   by such an elusive hoax.

The world revolves with countless
cosmic bodies in the great unknown
> or are we just going in circles,
> aimless and alone.

Ha, in me ancient death stirs no fear,
yet I shudder from the fact
> that the world will continue,
> business as usual, even without me here.

Yes, I'm bleeding,
but a question I maintain,
> Is it me, or is
> the rest of the world insane?

Warring

One bullet,
two bullets,
young soldiers
growing old

Hardened

As the sun rises, my resolve fades.
Its warmth seems to melt away
the bitter cold of anger that comforted me
while I slept in this endless bed alone.

He, the man sleeping on
the couch, knows his name has etched
a weak spot into my heart.
Arrogantly, he throws accurate daggers at it.
Target practice.

Morning brings joy,
but we have not emerged unscathed.
For that soft spot has hardened
ever so slightly as it
does every such occasion.

Amazing how one adapts
to her environment to survive.
And one of these mornings,

the sun will find me long gone.

An Ode to Grandma Dorothy

The dimensions of mortals too inept
to realize the miracles that form you
    and by what means you shine,
        brilliant in all your glory.

Even the seeds that grew from your rich soil,
watered by the tears of your ancestors,
    fail to comprehend your complexities.
    Flesh of your flesh, they carry your spirit,

one that has danced to djembe drums for generations.
Ogitsi*, a steadfast nurturer of e-lo-hi-no*, unwilling
    to be defined by man alone.
    I employ a thousand tongues to express

my gratitude for all you have given me.
Beyond the gifts you bestowed to my siblings
    and me, the only children in the ghetto with
    diamonds and fur coats, still greater than

the countless crayons and stuffed animals,
you lavished us with red kisses and lasting hugs;
    love that shapes a child into a wind of change
    indicative of dreams dreamt long ago.

I did not inherit your flare for fashion,
but I do reflect your deep-rooted cheekbones,
    and dignified aura that out-glistens
    any sequined hat. Take refuge in knowing

your legacy is eternal. Find solace in my thoughts
and prayers. My love for you escapes measurement.
    May the wonder produced only by God's
    grace and mercy mold me into at least half

the woman you are. And as the days and nights continue
to maneuver their way through time, and we get ensnared
    in this life that changes with wanton disregard, remember
    that Candis loves you a bushel and a peck.

God is.

---

* ogitsi – Cherokee for "our mother"

* e-lo-hi-no – Cherokee for "earth"

Unconcealed Cycle

It's an amazing feeling
That first time your man hits you

Not shock
But loss

The last of your innocence ripped from you
By the one who was supposed to protect you

The love of your life
The prince from your girlhood fantasies

In the flesh
He's just a man

Make the excuses
Cover up

Conceal
Concealer on to mask the bruises

Not the life you once imagined
Shrinking under the weight of his hand

Nothingness
Blank

You remember hiding under the table as your father,
Formerly a superhero in your eyes, taught your mother a lesson
For being so stupid and weak all the time

Now you watch as your love, your foe,
The father of your baby girl,
Holds her up and admires her before he gently kisses her

Sunshine in the Mourning

I mourned for my heart.

The tool that works so hard to keep me alive,

I'd lent it to another who left it devastated and struggling to survive.

I mourned for my mind.

The key that keeps me sane,

It was tampered with by a fraud, forced to calculate lies in vain.

I mourned for my soul.

The inner being that speaks on my behalf,

For it was voluntarily lured from its correct path.

I mourned for my spirit.

The gear that gets my wills turning,

It continues to run now simply because Rome is burning.

I mourned for my body.

The beautiful home in which I reside,

Once warmed by another's touch, now heated by pride.

I mourned for my virginity.

That held my worth tightly secure,

Lives on as a sweet memory, tainted and impure.

I mourned for my heart that has grown bitter,

I mourned for my mind that has grown cynically wittier.

I mourned for my soul that is charred from harsh lessons,

I mourned for my spirit that has relinquished some of its essence.

I mourned for my body that craves what will never be returned,

I mourned for my virginity, a trade-off for wisdom earned.

I mourned most for a love that was lost,

Unfulfilled potentials paid the cost.

I mourned because of my innocence's fall,

Bittersweetly knowing it's better to have loved than to have never loved at all.

Armor

Why do I revel in my own sadness,
I get there and I sit there,
Stewing in my own madness.

They say,
Don't let your path cross that of a black cat,
Well I came in direct contact.

It hissed then ran away,
That was last night,
So will ill luck play out today?

If I believed in that tricky scoundrel called luck,
Then I'd have a reason
As to why I'm stuck.

Wrongfully quarantined in a foreign desert,
Where I cannot grow,
Cacti sign fear and hope, but needles hurt.

I'm beautiful, I can stop wars with my smile,
I'm an adult,
But right now I'm a child.

I called my mother for direction,
Too far to rescue me,
But her voice was consolation.

I must slip mine off
And wear new skin,
Buy myself some tougher
Than what I'm in.

Failure v. Success

I'm afraid to try,
afraid to be wrong,
failure petrifies me.

I see it looming over my success,
I tuck my tail and lower my head,
hoping to move past it undetected.

But I know it will see me eventually,
swoop down on me, sink its
fangs into my weak flesh,
and suck the life right out of me
with little to no effort.

That's why I'm afraid to try.

Attempting to live one's dreams
presents the possibility of failure,
and my feeble heart
wouldn't be able to withstand
yet more disappointment.

So, I sit in false contentment,
silently resenting my cowardice ways.

But maybe, just maybe, it is not
the sting of failure that I fear,
maybe success is my true adversary.

My own strength and power frightens me.

Yes, that's it.
I'm afraid to try,
afraid to be wrong,
success petrifies me.

DrugLord

I am a soldier,
a warrior raging against
the machine that was constructed
to destroy me.

I am as fierce as my coal-complexioned
ancestors, as strong as their teeth
that gnashed at lions,
fists that traumatized enemies.

I'm a warrior with a sword
that spits flames,
burning the souls of
those who dare rise against me.

I am on a mission,
a dark yet noble mission,
to overthrow a system that exist
to keep my face in the mud.

Empowered by spoils yielded
from the earth, I am a warrior
with the means to reclaim the riches
stolen from me 400 years ago.

I am a defector dodging uniformed
demons that reek of swine,
I refuse to have a number
branded in my forehead.

Held captive and the ransom
is my soul,
which, though sullied,
maintains its value.

People say I am a thief,
I steal the innocence
of the youth, destroy families,
and poison bloodlines.

But I disagree,
for I am a warrior raging against
the machine that was constructed
to destroy me, take food from
my belly, land from beneath
my feet, and kill my offspring
before they have a chance at life.

I am a soldier,
a warrior with a dark
yet noble cause.

Job Justified

Let the wind blow through the broken pieces

Temporary reprieve from the burning sensation

Who dares question God

About the hell on Earth

For Earth shall no longer cover its slain

Blood penance for sins of man paid by the weak

His power is eternal

His wrath swift, vengeful

His grace and mercy bountiful

Quicken thy own spirit

Lest thou be curst amongst the wicked

Even in your righteousness

He will slay you

Yet trust Him

For He will be your salvation

Me in My Own Space

Snapshots of my spirit flow
onto the page

As creatures of my wilderness
roam uncaged

An unruly hour meanders outside
of its pre-determined limits

Stretching its limbs to places
beyond seconds and minutes

And there's just one witness

And for That, I Love You

I love you because you are the spark
that ignites my desire
to be a better human being

You open me
and turn me
towards the sun

A sun so bright
that it is able to find
every part of me,
even parts that I've hidden
in the deepest wells of my eyes

Your genius has figured me out,
you have navigated through
and conquered all of my complexities

You understand me
and for that, I love you

I do

My loyalty loves you too,
protective, it stands guard
beside you, reminding you
that I am forever yours

Your admirable wit
leads my intelligence
in an enticing tango

They dance so well together,
yes, so well do they dance

I love you because you respect
my virtue and hold it in your
hands ever so gentle,
carefully assuring me
that it's okay to be myself
in this world of conformity

You laugh at my corny jokes,
chastise me when foolishness
has blinded my better judgment,
and kiss away my tears of frustration

And for that, I love you

A Birthday Poem for Snook and Outlaw

We often hear talk of a woman's worth,
How Mother Nature begot the Earth.

But do we fully understand,
The power a woman holds in her hand.

She can calm the seas and send the war cry,
She can figure life's mysteries without asking why.

She can soothe a worn spirit and ease a troubled mind,
You confront the world boldly, because you know she's close behind.

One woman in particular is one of God's greatest gifts,
Count yourself blessed when you're in her midst.

This woman is a doer not just a talker,
No one other than Mrs. Lillie Bell Walker.

She keeps it cut-and-dry and gives it to you straight,
And won't hesitate to talk about you to your face.

"Baby, you need to lose a few pounds, get a haircut,
Leave that man alone, get on top of your stuff.

Remember who and whose you are,
Hold tight to God and you'll go far."

Hey, don't make the wrong move or let your tongue flip too fast,
Because tucked in her purse is an old Crown Royal bag *.

Grandma Lillie will congratulate your rights and scold your wrongs,
Then forward your business to the Pow Wow Club all night long.

What man dares to tame this shrew,
A Mississippi outlaw that's who.

Elijah Walker stepped up to the plate,
And declared her his helpmate.

Yeah, he lets her have her way and won't say much,
But he ain't gon' tolerate unnecessary stress and such.

"Now Beep Beep, this just ain't right,
Them folks grown, you can't control their life.

If they wanna act a fool then let 'em,
But don't let 'em raise your blood pressure.

Alright, just one slice, this pie should last,
Or else the next time Geraldine comes, I'm going to tell her about your goodie stash."

He's her rock, her friend, he's connected to her spirit,
He tells her the truth even when she ain't tryna hear it.

And it was this month, many years ago,
That God sent these angels to the Earth below.

Since then, they have grown, seen, and accomplished many things,
Which led to their union, confirmed by wedding rings.

These two are a royal pair,
Who will reign here on Earth 'til they ascend into the air.

---

* Inside family joke: my grandmother carries a pistol in that bag

Venom

Kisses sweet
Words bitter
Poisonous is his sting

Causing slow death
Rot from the inside out

Reoccurring exposure to the venom
Yet no immunity acquired

Light dims
Beauty fades
Heart strings coming undone

Causing fatigue and self-abjuration
Resentment from the inside out

Anonymous

Body scarred…
Ego bruised…
Soul resilient…

Sacrifice

My cries of defeat
grovel humbly
at my Savior's feet

Though I never birthed you
you are a part of my legacy

Father, Son, Holy Ghost
the trinity is complete

www.ingramcontent.com/pod-product-compliance
Lightning Source LLC
Chambersburg PA
CBHW032210040426
42449CB00005B/528